praise for

Abraham Smith & *Insomniac Sentinel*

"This message from the kinetic yet ghostly realm of Wisconsin that suffuses Abraham Smith's Insomniac Sentinel alive with its rural glossary, with its hidden waking clandestinely complex within seeming quotidian display. It scripts a lingual fuse of heresy, that absorbs particulates of human brewing, and what follows is a slow magnetic glow that suffuses the text not unlike a susurrant under-ringing. Thus, it emits by complexity by this glow letting us know that verbal life continues to not only thrive but quietly erupt and cascade from regions that we seemingly thought to be inert, always poetically aware of yielding circuitous treasure from what was thought to be a less than magnetic hamlet."

— **Will Alexander,** Pulitzer finalist for *Refractive Africa*
and author of *The Contortionist Whispers*

"you know, i am the giver/back of sound." This bardic claim could only be true of Abraham Smith, who sings open-throatedly the continuous song of a crane lifting off the junkpile and into history's storm. His song pushes through and around the language of working, of working bodies, both human and inhuman, raising it all up, illuminating it, as in a manuscript, indicating what is precious, as if sound could be the one thing it is not, and shed light. That's the sad note in this "gravy-to-cradle" threnody, this "lunged-up thud tender." Reading Abraham Smith makes you ask the big questions, like, are our wings made of the shreds of where we came from? Does a bird fly on its wing, or on its song?"

— **Joyelle McSweeney,** author of *Toxicon and Arachne*

"I can hear Abraham Smith's voice intoning in his breathless and headlong fashion throughout his latest collection of poems. The verses practically read themselves to me, accompanied by an insistent rhythm a backbeat for music that these poems conjure up."

— **Charlie Parr,** Smithsonian Folkways recording artist and author of *Last of the Better Days Ahead*

"Abraham Smith is one of my favorite living poets keeping the art form alive. He is patiently stoking the fires of imagination and his persistence has kept the cinders of inspiration smoldering. It is a joy to read his work and thrill to hear him read it in person."

— **Margo Price,** Grammy nominee, Farm Aid board member, and author of *Maybe We'll Make It*

INSOMNIAC   SENTINEL

INSOMNIAC SENTINEL

poems

Abraham Smith

BAOBAB PRESS

First Printing

ISBN-13: 978-1-936097-44-9
ISBN-10: 1-936097-44-3

Library of Congress Control Number: 2022941858

Baobab Press
121 California Ave
Reno, Nevada 89509
www.baobabpress.com

Cover Image: "Cranes in their vigalance" appears in the *Harley Beastiary*

For Yam Sir: October 6 2007 - March 18 2018
& & & & & & & & & & & & & & & & & & &
For Crawdaddy: April 25 1970 - December 2 2013

CONTENTS

"These crayons fly"

—Lorine Niedecker

THE INSOMNIAC SENTINEL

that's my buddy brother-in-law eddy
on nights at the paper mill
last night fell he says

asleep standing up je-
sus the machine
could've eaten you

nah he says honest worst
would have happened
the paper would have broke

right square where i fell
or it was the facer we
were making

and that's a pretty
heave it mess it's a leap in
the hay see

whether facer or no
all to a man jump
in and down and

shoulder that
snake of steaming slop
back up out over to

another it's a vat where
it's time to cut the broke up
and cook back to usable

cook it back to usable
there are guys there guys there
can tell it just looking at it

when it's ready to be facer again
changed is what any body says
given time and activities

smeddy's face ilk ug
icked round y
inters f rinks

say we no man left behind ever
and puff a chest and suck a
gut in but of course we do

lose ourselves and
others connections
concessions rusting

carts of sparks
pistolwhipped
arc to ground

in popeyed veteran
in bitter flag popping loyal
in laurel royal alloy say

to a fault shined knights
in peaty books through the so much
rain blasts their underclothes

to rusts hued for good
call it mettle's happy heart attack
let by sunset atmosphere

digging at his arm eddy is
where fiberglasses little
glass mouths biter cottons

candy flea facer
rashed him up good
into battle now goodly noble

knights came to expect to endure
how herald's heft burned the shoulder
blade to flame cranes grey graven

stands one among many there
she alone the steady eddy one up on
one 'rina foot while silent roundly shining

in the other weathervane birdpaw basically
it's a manna snowcone minimoon held up
crystal ball style and the legend goes

should she drop that upraised stone of light
in her shadow's shallow into water's lax glass lap
then sleep felled she waked better be

by footstone spats with waters
dimpler cymbaler wrinkler surprise her
flat out needs be brought around

to home fires vigilant ligament villagant stay
tuned to any twig's neck hex say because not in this
alone because next bird up just won't do

because spoiled milk twice boiled
slips down the storm gutter pant of the son
of the father hey eddy

hey maybe
that's a wad of paper
facer i mean

steaming and staring and stirring up
through upraised heraldic crane
say she footballed the broke

balled your own one face maybe
so lips race eyes to nose sew
yr brows like fire starter sticks say

rubbed together patch the parachute say
with little snails of smoke say
little ferns unfolding say

on cicada's swale-you-whole-womb-tomb say
on cricket's bandy-knee-shriek say
in every 3rd bird's skipping 7inch say say

say sleep truth escapes no
one she does drift
does drop you

coinwise falling in
slip stream glassy your
second name releasing below

ah tell now how time's a river impulsive to the sea
or what's time's scuttle when yr under with no
real bellow gill to plum blossom bosom straining

say seconds days say before grapes
before melon fire eyes bigging
for she sudden sight sees you

as maybe no one
ever has quite
see-seed you

bottomed backed trembled you
solo sexing it you
getting born or first trying to

sign your name while the current's scrawl
does nothing much with you and you're watching
her peace sign peace sign foot falling for you

drawling inevitability of a machine
closing and clasping and raising you up out
you gasping you sputtering you coughing drool dew

bap tisk lee east new you new
saved the day she did and you
ya saved yr life's chandelier bandito sound for

her sing after won't you it's your throat so
stretchered to those hundred thousands gathered
as around a brown tomb upset

sing black cat
sing somewhere down the road
sing bottle up a tree

hey every eye a fish
fat with gold
made to measure you

hey every wriggler can't span
when song hunger huges louder
than shouting gun chorus

when every mouth swells
to glitz yr king fame name
precious metal fork to spade

to tnt to plodding
dozer how much then
after under might remain

gonna dig up into sidehill's
subsidence gonna cove an ear
to badger heart or bear thump

thump it's not the rain's choice
it's the roof's arrhythmias after
o doe o drolling drops

like god does
god does
teeth to babies

dearer than marrow in a doll
that's ether's zero only
well met helmet of the ortolan bunting

that's the pike the drool town raven is
rowing when above this
river's varicose roll

that's the river keeping everything going
that's the paper the facer rolls deafening on
that's that equator heat belting off the driers

takes the edges
off the porno
mags up in to a sneary little curl

o worthy o consider your own glowing
stone phone on nights like these at the mill
your weight in gold now what might that be

would it yr weight or
you and your children
or you yr children and your wife

or you yr children your wife
and your truck needs a new alternator
or would it you yr children

your wife your truck needs a new bearing
and yr bent cussing the pigweed the gutcut
wound so tight around the tines

the batters of the rototiller as to be
tumor woodstone workerback
o broken clock of weeds

or do you weigh goldenwise
what the minnows in
the mountain streams weigh

tipped and slipped and
running wounds
debt dogs keep callin

may grow cleaner
keener the closeness
to sources

may that's after
april before june and all 3
render we rectangular

better call 'em what they are
slippy timothy onion lard
oblong internal flame dirts

bucketed down upon
our negligible heads
and time has a way now

of singing the high
end at the start part
o bottlerocket aimed

more or less away
o lizard in a blue jay tonight
o boom baboomboom tonight

surprise now come to find now
has a price pray eagle river of coffee
keep me in seeing eye stones tonight

in the other shoe dropsy stall
in sandstorms of sound stones tonight
in lichens shot out shotguns

pray get up get up run
good greeny mouths
thru starguts some

cheek gardens forged
them blue fords forever
blue turd smoke turnin

out warmin tailpipes
easy as blueprints
for bratwurst factories

where no poisoned dogs
ever lie kicking snow gonna
stuff 'em with good guys

go by nicknames moodring
their tempers and it's only
in summer wait you'll see

gallant passions improvised
in winded tattoos whose
greener blues don't quite

THEY PAINT

themselves
with mud
and the afterlives

of certain pondy ass plants
and they accomplice 'at
with a whole lot of throwing

stoop and pitch
stoop and pitch it
stoop pitch and

what can't ya see
can feel it falling
but there again

you threw
it so you
are it

just as the pirate eyepatches
tarantulaing yr lapel
are who you've sometimes been

just as the weather
was the one
weathered the weather

hi-5 blind
cool killing it
oh so casual in the win

carrion confetti
of coleridge chris
whitley christopher smart

rain trellis luck marks
mud orthodontics
mist posthumous mist

under these and they i glaze
and praise run and runnel
stoop to stipple in arts

of camouflage try
transference kind travels
try blind sides lined

with snowflake catpaw
with newspaper ember
with moth blow

yr nose
with a hamburger
napkin

kid killed it
so wipe it
fresh from the heart

all
upon
him

and what did he learn
from the body undone
that dead wet

life in it heady
heat weak wane unready
echo pre shout

gravy to cradle
settled up past flung
lunged under thud tender

blocky punctuation
a den a dean a black eye
everywhere on the body

nowhere in open air
i recall my self boy
uneven shit yard

that's them dogs for you
that's throw a ball up
for catching it

that's trickier than
you might think
that's something to do

with the tragic joke
slant and slope
of self and earth

acned acre boy
in the ditches
kickin mt dew

bottles pregnant
with pisses
pump my arm

wild god mad
guttin insulation
from ghost cupboard cups

now that trucker he might
milk plunger his horn
conquistador beard blatz

might flight a flat
rock sound
clap those tasky erasers

whited with ash
from human bone burned
clap and the harnessed ghosts

and the cliff divers
and the meth freaked freds all
to a one fingertips touch fall

that's self same thing about dogs
thinks it's all about them
my god good errant toss

my bad dog good pirate prince
my shitty spit slobbered ball
my 29 tosses til dryish again

my not my ceiling opens
my not my sky uncorks
my not my season tumbles

as carpish suckers
roiling in shallows
but how can i track you

if you ain't workin
on something hard
unheld greenbrowed

water reopens and
they're there as it does
skirting us lonesome hihat weavers

and ringing silence
lawless and binding
ringing it with a double u

all lamppost future pure
and woven of such
wrack as this as they

covered up in it
hunker nestward
their blood the hunter's

supple
clay slow
blood

their ladder
snorts the checkered adder
bade the chokecherry aubade not me

their pliant cattail body
bossy bleed note redwing
come sterling stopped atop bows

at the paces
of watchfulness
for the prices of love

for we taste of one
another swallow the
oldest urges to hum

flake cereal commercials
cattish cartoon sugars
wall pity shivers

have the courage
of half a burying
have worm pencil ear

have yr funeral all
planned out on down
to the moist towlette

have next life sketched
uuu loose little copepods
eaten twice by turtle eyes

SHELL LIFE

a shallow curve
racetrack oval
through it

one
hatchling one
walling

dale
dale
dale

seedspring bedspring
faster flower
karo rag fire

lost her rambler
morseling the pound
sign off caved

payphones
playground lunatic
wafers strangely

kneecap scab his
for want's
dialtones that's one

shear tablecloth
up over cliff's edge
leading lip mess

popping boys
locker rooms
sinister towels

fuss veil full beat
young bum comes
right out

hatch man
that's some
excellent reckless prep

for seed kill days
and nights
days and nights

wanton craps dice
throw and throe
them bones-ing that

riot curve wall
dead same as
sexy sex

most
people
want

hammered at
flounce the animal
peeks or rears

aside a spell
set self one
minute's epic year

often gravely
misunderstood
for my inveterate

gentleness
one such suckling
leveret me

grass bend hips
mine born rusting
burnt opal crushed gold

sometimes now mother
crane she'll
scan the leavings

she'll low
and lance she'll
up and gargle

she'll down
potato art
smashed by

her rowdy
lifer she'll
eat the shell

lightbulb
icecream
eucharist bell

paint chip
fly twist
paint chip

wonder while she
angels upward
spent shell rattling

how she
sounds
to herself in

ramble shambles
up there? you
rat slapdancin

plastic riding
over fetid
insulation

you glad adder
handmade handsome ladder
hammered by deep high times

you rungs ones
filament ex-
posed tooth

militant seaplant
wild root
boo booth

seek a plastic
plant for shade
for dog for shame

turned on our
red fat hero bat
when antler

proved light-
ning prays
to stony stone

for walkers
on all four guts
lined clover green

when antler
sapling granite
all the way

wish glass
held fast
same

corks not
stoop cool
no more

gauzy resolutions
mob gobs absolute
the coldest you can get is

corpse dressed down
in a coat of
echoes of echoes

in a wet web of
woulda coulda
going to

in a dream worsted
stow phrase ever
sickly sweet

pillow road kill case
lumped up in
the silence between

every other road car
expert dead meat flies
drearer than the bees

materialize their lives
candy comb conical
beady ash embering

steely wool to
grater put sparks
lights like love

fish gasp
in other centuries roar
ragged fire

cat sing door spring
buzz head meth head
sweethearting the screendoor

no time
no money
to deal

and the weather
careless laughing
from the west

the broke patch
the broke car window
with plastic grocery bags

yeah wind's
juiciest pleasure ever
probably is fucking

with halfassed
expediency
and fustianly

blats black
heavy waters fire
given any green speed

save the milk-
blood school
zone one

the sound of yr
sometimes father
when young

and begging
for gum oh why
don't you just chew

on your tongue
pulled harder
than any sucker fish

your kite
you're kidding me
god's lit eyelid fluttering

wanting to hold you
in its high hole
heaven did or sky

DOUBLE VISION

ah when new baby rises
rises up all black out drunk
from curbstones seafoamed

in false crests of
newspaper and trashed
xmas wrapping paper

rises up in a coast
or crust of bread
coat trench

something so all leg
so old and new rises
rocks along

this land here
times ago
that ocean

this new thing
proofs it
that muddle throttle

murk at sound
of yr own voice
applaud when

they applaud
to plod upon
applause's plaudits

for lauded yourself
saliva string
a ropetow between

moth from the mouth
of the nameless goner
and day's first rooster

shovin a frozen flame catkin
up under
saggin saint tent

of dawn what is it
to throw yr blood
up in cask air ask rooster

why baby decides
megadeath for song
plunks the button

with one oafish thumb
plain rain down along
windseam bird crown

or capable or culpable
or cups of fate
spluttering are we

when the train
wags east old hitchyard
whited with styrofoam

lends chainlink some teeth
wide man stooped up to squatting there
blows a coffee in near

car wreck tires
talking and writing
shriek black

from his ass
sailing out now
in vague parable parade

baby the second towers
nearer second first
needle for a nerve

behind deadline seamstress mowing
airplane smoke stitches
in kin to kitsch sackcloth

and with the mercilessness mind
of one acid's say
baby 2 rainin blowholes

in face scapes of baby 1 til
like an ages old dipper whose
dip spit wears a hole in chin lip

ah habit's holes
try and muddy over
with egg crates

snake bite hammer time oil well
snake hammer bite oil time well
snake time hammer bite oil spill

from dear dear beak
from almost a drink
this spine so liqui-new

babe breath prized
mincin and particular real anger
chipdust pinched by one fatso leerer

unborn again number 1 is
ancillary rooms darkening
click it and the life

cord sags again against
shilled earth bad nite
dill plant no match

for the ceo
done with his
cigar sun and

i have heard the mighty
misty professors
to pull at their sugar beards

at their usual salt bangs
crazy bard
hard over

this fam kill astonishment
but with no real reasonable or
okay words to peal

their knowall whereall gone with silent
earth up under stacked wood
and i have read plenteous loud

psych books piled unto the kingdom
about how you are
how you are because

the pissed and percussed upon
middle child your
first born wavin a flamin

signature's vowels
bulging distended
corrals younger

kitten blood
in a bedbug
tadpoles

in a cistern
turn the waters
clearer only

child tether fizzing
down the dynamite
tricked up plenty

by the last born
all surveillance gone
i slip to the podium

in this tide tweed shined by
rain and time rot am i not
before yr very first memory

every hill every river
every drumlin every shale
every edge to vanish ever stone over

every talus slipper
every plains whose windsong
mitts to copping fire

river run beat teeth deep
acclivity sharp crushed glass
escarpment's echo descrying

rib rill rises flats fats ridges
there where the sib plot thicked thicker
than mule spit after a day

stuff was glue you could hand down
to a kid for the pleasure
of a hollow hour filled

shake it out cross the yard
mule drool throw it up uhoh
ya stuck it in a tree and

with nobody tall enough home and
with all the ladders down the road
as they and they was pitching in

at painting barns redder
leaves you kid jump jumping
the feather piston of yr breathin

but there is no way is no way
all yr hope goats squeezed
'gainst fence wind dragging

those luscious shorthair
grasses just a little
left right left left

BRAKE 4 CRANES

for their size
is ours
or close

anything you love
blow it all
your size or close

i love maudlin turquoise
earrings okay one
your size or close

i love cape cod beech leaves
in early oct toothache bright
okay one your size or close

i love tea on my teeth in the cool pm
and to be near a dim lit bathroom okay
one your size or close

i love wearing a hat in a house
and running hot water over ever redder hands
for winter's sacre sake okay one your size or close

i love it when i check email
and there are none no not one
okay one your size or close

i love sticking my neck out
for unjust people with green eyes
okay one your size or close

calls theirs cull sack
debt natal stay-cation
for a trachea call their

unison dandy leek call their
pond jump when kid jump call their
wastey corn teeth laughed free lichen icon their

unicycle bard call their
union pant sauce call their
fascia skeet trashcan lick call their

acne cream squeegee dream call their
blown knee brace ace rage call their
hand pump the well honk geek call their

dirtin curtain dinosaur call their
heartpine stage planks repurposed as
dolls for wet herdsman call their

only way to get that wet
is ya don't wait on the river call
culdesac neck unspill

one good place is
to raise a family my good friend's kids
bored wd rub wheels to

curbs upon giving skateboard's
unmistakable trenchant
construction patter cranes

so lovelovely in their til death ardor
in the land of tammy
wynette well met why not hurt yr

hands a little for their ardor arbor
already a stout copse just and standing
thick lush beside sparer coppices

gaptooth haha eye-crept
thru spindles over air
apple green shoulders

into the pissin internet where
rapt injectable plastics enhance mints
in the fleshy mouths of scorchin deportees

die for you die for you
die for you die for you
die for you die for you

died in willy
shakespeare
times ago

tho these midwestern thespians strut
and rill this rehearsal hall still
sound about if

enunciation
were a runrail judge's
florid bile

and pedantics
a kit you try and trace force
with drunk thumbs

after midnight on
what once was
christmas eve sir

about like if an oxfordian's oars'
suspended richmond drips got pinched by
some soil cap scholar layin by

erased blunders for eyes
hangover incurable matter
salted or egging

so rubs old ink river
into his gored tomato gums
sees didn't i tell you heracliteanly

pisses a fail to
arrive at sea
sit me down this forest dim

as tho low
in hull the water
my mouth tightening

between the pine
and woodpecker
crosshatched in flight

that i might listen to
heart's time is its own
horse swallowing

is a man moanin
through leaves
doubletime and there

s/he is
lean against trees
the ones too big for their own

britches lord that's
a sycamore one those
what they call born nudists

and the sick leaves
in their taperings
sort of like ready

to fuck you up
bout the size of
an ancienter shame

give him away sheepish
pelt in a creek eyes
takes that taint off

sweat to a future smear
child ups to reachable window
where one passing man with both eyes

is seen to be wretched in lampshades
powered by his dog whose coloring
conjures a country yam calm

where the bombs
sweaters slipped over shiverers
where the thoughts steady

in heads rung
sponged and bestowed
a not uncertain warmth

where the human
humaning again
where pliable domino turns

purblind pures
this where patience is
and angry ain't and

if cloned coins colors
of breaths breathed
by cloths buried then

no more sweet lingerer
columbine freely
climbs herself

s-
  o-
t-
  h-
e-
  r-
e

NATOMY

they will kite and key over
tallest mountains
snow jag hiss kind

heart monitor in heart
attack's welly foam kind
and they will with the eases

of phrases strike
you in the belly
of the bell

wcw purrin beauty
obliterates
authority

hank baitin pinched vinegar
purple bruise fruit bird
perception unction and

my reading all that
in susan howe and
maybe somehow

splicing johnny keats in
puts me in mind
of folks giving birth to overalls

back when brass clasp
fell on off an amniotic tongue
some power wire undoved

bless the ragged
vinegar sputter of a back-
glancing heart

you know i am the spanner of spaces
you know i am the giver
back of sound

in methy rentals
on dug skin
their bones hangers

seems they step on slips
cast off bad water
in movies when she

she's running
for her
dark life

when the metal ploughs come in
the people were sore afraid they'll
poison the soil the accented said

no sir just gonna steek to my
wud one offered one old bohunk
his skin so moled by sun

you'd have thought the day
had a hidden behind ear
number 2 pencil had a hidden

test and was bubbling in
C C C C C spinning circles
closed in him

spat tar
nicking it
in to him

always heard that'd get you
least most of the way to
not that far from average

hate to say it but it's to crane
credit the chemicals on credit killed
the fields same russet deathlife hillsand

shoehorn scissor
shotgun crane mouth
bellow tomato beanie

above rope or straight smoke neck
above last year's wasp's nest blown
one stop shop stab and done shuttle the hack

down smoke rope
held to oval then
for one fledge of tocks then

fuel to forge force bird sky worthy
your fate to go down
something 2 carrots thin

plastic bag in elm arm alarm
coked up man's fixity eye
i go where the night leads me

says slapping at his pockets
like money fights
flights or bites

when scissors and
shoehorns get busy together
with rope and old waspnests

there you have my
memorex of my whack ass
stepdad cutting my hair on

the yard missing cuttin my ears
off barely carcass flies over
a county off comin runnin

cuz the baste sang
oh i ain't got no
turkey flats no

and i knowin then
the bleedout secret
freshet candle humalong

someone swimming
flying fulsome whim water
the milk peace in all glide

seam gem wise water
midswim mind and then
icicle carrot gat and then

gargle gargoyle and then
gaggle gag gull and then
on into the blown

waspnest bulb belly body
probably half alive still pre lift
but then what would you be for

if we are all a little or a lot
a woodlot one good load
what would you be for what

mess i vote for
let my pretty
my petty parts scatter

cross the platte's
skimmy
bends

many or one
footbridge footage
jitterbulge floating

until
a toll
atoll

cu-
rr-
ent

sw-
all-
ow

fi-
sh
whip

worse overtime
friend than wings
past dawn

unto the waste corn
walked off the job
those statues just did it again

ah history we
try and stone it
sand bleeds

WHY DANCE

ask mom
ask mom
ask sister

ask sun lost
on a powerpole ask
moon in a mess

of wires
ask dove's
asthmatic jelly

strapped to
overdone toasts
no know sans do

sure lean
like cranes do
like that

like sap
in saplings does
like that

like the
hungover do
like that

brain fixin
to fall
from yr nose

yes
maybe
so

the nose an antique iron
foamed with rust
thence to doorstop turned

yes
maybe
so

my prayer
may everyone one
possess juicy uses too

highly unthought out
across summer lakes
89 damselflies pantomime time's

shiver frisk the shower has
an asshole and
that is called the grate

or drain
the hungover have eyes
like scribbles like drains like grates

gratis just
don't happen
much these days

all the free bins
sticky with spills
murmur dismember drunk sleep

all the lost and founds
floated into sexted corners
fella coroner's first met dreams

alive and beaning little
ragged blood notebook
sheets yanked hasty

so snowy edges snaggle dang
so pages sump blanks some stained
why must we mind it so

our one beautiful body
gym made fades
damage leading beauty

by the nose i know a showy
hole in the new oak
leaf oval soft grrr

at rabbit ran dream
elapsed thunder
razzed condom it's a reach

and there's
now for
nothing too green horn

their dogtired stances
in spring in fall
just taking it all in

while the fire
in the wing eases off
off and down

crane bone
corn bone
beau light one

do so
holy loomer loom
best bent spent hanger ever

too slight to ring or
take instruction ticks
wisper than ghost birds

picketing for seeds
upon the junked banks
of the laughs of the spiteful

curbs blacked tired kissin
drunkards' babyface wheels
catfish licorice lupus creels

it's dark and it's cold and it's real
bound car lock curse it
curse them smug keys glinting

then a wing tilts
ear of an elephant
a la the arm of a swimmer

catching sun
catching at sun
catching the sun and

they're at it again
could have been a cork-
screw grouses the plough

i could've been
just depends
you know

upon the mold if cyclone
man that's some third shift whinin
could've been a stingray

preens the cork
with the one red end
after the laughter dies down

called to fake a fate late
or faded foot upon the wall
one antediluvian rolly holer

trodding my calling
i go to war
nothing

but the one red end
and a saying ascribed to mystics
addicted to petunia light

coocooing my lips
corks stop flow lord
so pure to one thing

can't cop
natural
to a little range

some army beige
some safari khaki
some cirrhotic amarilla

some ten hundred
thousand wino corky eraser bits
pinch pink jingo this here floor

while half a noun
sick with gravity ah and
mellow as a pencil drawn tool

dozes no lowers itself down
the oldest man
he don't so much sit as fall

for the oldest lawn chair
what strength he has
is in his arms

fishing for crappies
with tent poles cadged by
nutso wind chair

wet dream of a ruined
badminton birdie chair
was in guinea he was there

against the japanese
snipers in the trees
kicking up split dust

buddy billy beside no
behind no drunk on bull-
ets unwinds electric shorting

last asleep he's his own now
belly blade only times
lifts a little like the lizards do

bullet in the face remembers
and doesn't like crying
backwards the tear searing in

his one and only other eye
out out and that's just
the beginning at that time

every nurse young thin beautiful
halfa head fillin fuller in time
come on back home in time

he was at war saw action
but one day in time
memorial day '18

he's 95 and 93 days he
can still salute then
they pop off rifles

there's a mural downtown
they just finished that
he looks like himself likes that salute

pop off there is truly a motion for everything
something called milking muscle memory
wide i watch the sun bind wind

and chat with aspens a candy spray
watch moth and butterfly
play fake fall leaf on vetch and mallow

on buttercup on columbine
sheep babies bow true
their tails in circles spurting

i think to amuse the ewes
cough up more body patience
every being bending now

towards hunger
or plunder or caulk
or creek or creak o lovely love

loyal is as loyal does
eats the eyes off reason
the blood in me the blood in you

the bamboo the aspen and
what you get by on i get by on
the doling and the doffing

the witting wetness when
money was liquid metal
think low wing

'fore minting
think rayness
afterthought rifle's

endless rote
thorax peephole
could use ya a peony

preachin the good
jitters to the holy
hollyhock unstaged

do the hive tree
do tornado big spit
do the thrown thorn milk ballet

do 3am
phonebooth fulla
menus and wind and

all the gym socks
and gym shoes
and bloods

of the hawk
burst mice come
join this field

is a mold bread
this thinbone kneads
to scraps the want

to be anything
let me be good
bum today

let what is happenin
happen again already
and no shame

RIVER BLUES

back before forever was
back when time was light
and weather was no nebraska

to the not platte
go for safekeep
and quaff up

back when just
seed just dream rise
just rise just fall

ah pass through
decent peace saplings
a sudden ass grove of wimpy

from skyvault cupped they down
to stilt upon quieter
arbor and lumber

witch whim light
wind storm acomin
vacuums 'em again on

peaceways mostways til feathered
humans in sacrosanct parsimony
longin for a longbone tune

flute natural to one leg
furniture more whistle
o get on down in the carve

and holes yonder come
wagoneers in fire facemouth glut
from hitched post

to rippin machines in
a fuckin dart ate on a dare of time
stuffed the fartin steer

bulk quick corn rocket
ribbons the internals
fissures flesh in

a quicksand of fatty
in a deafen of
instable knacker

got a hoof on a
blue glue gun and
shut that rider up

in a quicklime of i am
be like if a piggybank
glued in 89

hundred different ways
skinny white overpour
sallow light no way tall seams

be like worms up
through a rain
chew and chew

steer you into
steer stare
ah art what ya et

after fall heart hamburger
hamburger guy hamburger car
brown car duh

light red
in a red rain uh
in a cowtown named

for a saint
shot in the neck
then snaking arrows

flower from him
in vermillion
calligraph caspers

a number drone
a letter shone
a musical note whimpers

played without heart
blurs to the belly button screw
in dead letter email addy

distracted as anyone is
not having a heart attack
and passin from switchin glow

to twitchy glow while the water
dwindles and the platte narrownecks
and the funeral cars gather

in the church lot
for gerald ox my ass
pure gazelle bred to work horse

in his drag rig
at the airport
got that thing up

near 200 mph long
landin strip in 19 and 53
see things built up quick

whole country
had that corn logic
concerning world war 2 and after

them short hair correct fellas
come back and prat around peaceful
for a 9 year say layby or so

but if you know a veteran
you know a volcano
in a teapot

refreshments plenty of
free parking
local boys

makin good get them race cars
off the streets go on and hero yr
hero hoodlums likes to say

come for the family entertainment
an obscenity of straightness
and it's just how much

fuel you can push through
and burn up quick relates to
wheel blear and burn kids

instinctive hands to ears
it's a war jet cousin kiss
in good fun

winner went straight fastest
and the folks all went home
little ringin in their ear

cursive unknotting down
along that intern tambourine
but they shut down the airfields

and i don't know seems like
folks just get busy doing something else
you mean out by the old sandplant

no i am talkin about the gravel pit
employs 9 guys go like bats out
of the good book i know cuz my cousin

rents out that way and she says
you can't hear yourself blink
for all that gust bust mack truckin

and she says at the morning
coffee or dishes it don't matter
the time of day you can watch

those trucks bomb down
the road or the roadcrews
puttyin the road holes opened

by the weight and bustle
of it all be it the potholes
drooled shut or just

them guys bustin
down the road and bustin
the road and she knows

one of 'em pretty good
dated him a good year
junior '77 can still

taste going down on him
after homecoming when
she was just stars and

honeyboats about the guy
and she still she still
guesses which one's him

can see his light his light turn
green on facebook around
when his truck veers

bitches at gravel borders
along the edges takes
out commando style

little pooch of pigweed parsnipcow
or three and she told off her kids
it's evil to drink tapwater

out of a squirtgun hates
that that homecoming
memory flashes both

thoughts one time taste
was hay needs digging out
the animals stand on too long

like if piss kissed
boredom into a hawaii new car
what's a snowplow to do in spring

the deceit of conceit of time
it don't pass and pass it
easies then leaps like a sex maniac

too long you stand
can forget anything
temporary by look in

the frigerator he went on
to two kids never hitched
wears his corn advert hat

just the same way those eyes tho
bulge more lord that ass fat
had to have somewhere to go

like he's pregnant way
he sort of negotiates
his guts around the subway eatin lite

in the new year be it steam hole after
the road crew gets gone
or these swirls of dust

comin up off gravel
truck beds she can't resist
that yellow line

runnin up her spine
narcissist dog runnin and
pissin at the same time

o some a ghost to u i post
a whiff puff up and tall
and forward and streaming

post it up in and out
of angel season seems like i
see cranes in everything

lonely as it gets out here push send
where there's no blockage
to where i might eye pop

wouldn't be surprised
maybe depending
i could see one of my people

back in the day married into astronaut
i am not tellin you anythin new
spit in a vial and they send it

back 77 percent bohunk 9
percent germane english and
the rest a song so unmannered

for a bird to lung expose
see every let loose
builds a mildew room and a back

alley down which larches
man slow put pout on whiskey
was it '71? came a knock at

the door last day of february
all the soft valentine candy
bust a tooth by then

i open the door and
i shit you not
redheaded stranger

bird was like what is up
and we just stood there
glued up in gogo eyes one

and one until i think i freaked
and she jumped faulty back
like a shit metal walmart

bookshelf we put together
drunk forgot
the crucial screw

darlin this great wide
world can't you see us now
losin crucial screws

or stoopin for fallen ones
and once yr pockets fill
the mouth'll have to do

say a sturdy turning thing hum it
say a bulwarked mountain west
of here say a methless nebrasky

say a tweakless omaha
say a bright eye black
say johnny rash eyes smokin one

on a softboard porch
retired his goof dust machete
whisper it no nuke no nuke

no corny name to boot
no pretty vintage dangerous
cursive lifeless inside

no she i turns
turns to shut the door again
against red light green

and there and there again
in private rib little float to it of
ah well what else

offwhite wing
elbowin in
crestin in

while all up and down
her i throat
green peas

peas and pearls
precious squishes
loggerheads doggerel

by curds of light taken in
by move just it's all
a circuit throw

that switch there
that crane for walkin cane
step and she i steps

call and she i calls
stoop and she i stoops
there's a hole

mind the skunk skull
there's a knob nee
mind the cram ram proud obstinate

and there's moving sky pleases
yes the echoing twin
arrows through it yes

cuts and sutures by sound
from scar back to wound
from wound back to baby

from first scream to
a dark silent noise
little skundrunk sway

to the homecome slapblind
swear sweet hand reach for
pup pulp pulse hand

swear to it on a stack
like a deer head
skint alive

nor did we accept roamin
charges or were even ever aware
of our body clothes roasting

back then first darks
went softer and smaller
see wet rub long sparks

swear to it on a stack of jokers
so thirsty we thumbnailed open
dandelion leg lives and nursed

in seasons before
internet insulin
palm pilot porn

dirty hard dud
farm schnoz ghost oats
dirty hard dud

is was once was
lol fml lol fml
fml lol lol lol

IN TIMES OF LOVELY LOVE

out of or into the honest
random damn dandy blue
cranes jump feet straight 12 up

because they feel like it they feel it
because love is a juiced elevator at the bone
because love is this shined bell get at 'em

with glimmer and the marigold fable
y'all fairing and craning
at the metallurgic moon

brute spins the wooden mallet
and brute's baby child
does one grass blade the same

and town and city
they splay
so touchless these

opiate shit pinch days
share but one tiny and tittering
meltface fentanyl willkill T

hitches his played out town jeans
wets lips stoops a little bad back his
lady her capable arms

folded over her belly
is she called cold nah prow calm
warms bloods hers gentle as

hairs upon arms flow
foeless unto a liquid level spits in hands
looks up looks down

it's his working way of breathing
he's right there all of him at the broke
machine at the lovebreaking into her

3 add 9 hard laughs
2 plus 12 minus 2 sprinter's piston puffs up
and 6 and 6 of sorrow's kittens cracking grin

after grin to pine god
gets so old now
but not as old as old sheets

or unwashed jeans
the purchase of yr first
washing machine being what it is

to fall in love
with humanity again
lightbulbs being immoderate stupid

lampshades being decorative useful
maybe i want to tear on in and
mouth the burning runs a little chalky dry

via that char chew lure look on people
clicking off as they enter in
to duty being nine times

out of ten one poison river
the belltower fish gunner up
and did you further know the leap

these cranes accomplish
gets rushless as the oldest trees
old man traveling flag long pole

sap slow up pug's pug
sucking a halls the older doctor purrs
are you sitting leper leather

leaping cept with wings
saliva swallow sleet in sleep
legless eggless egress oaken

root to oaken
trunk to oaken
bough

oak oak once up in
i want that fortune
for how i future

long time no sea
how's yr salt intake been my sweet
guess alright

traveling mucho
writing much you are reading it
oak oak

grieve that druidic tic
tombwise in
so long

one such travailing
love bug
pikes he turns

oaking oaking
12 ticks up
per anno

attend a pendant ski to parasol
see vein must first low a pole
through leaf's heart

see the human eye trees
what i name spineway vein
one winter one presiding

breath bone tense reps green
it's a vascular brocade babe
and it's easy now on earth

to forget our bones
if not for dogs
no cows come home

magnetized by their own cud hearts
dogs do lazy like shruggin teens
little heels of green brown dust

eddy via muzzles in shade
in rhythm time to church
organ pedals pushed

through mahogany hymns
by rising bridge waters nosed
into brightest bridal car cans

not yet clear
of the heat of
hurrahing mouths

clinking sparking
the two pick up speed
chlorine in the hottub insane

fear thrall of copper wire thieves
of storm's leaves pansy daisy
clover nellie button sue

promissory clabber
debt vet cudgel
stomach gentle giant 4

paper ships airbrushed on green
paper ships nodding
at advances of water

twitching like that what does
one dog dream gone alone
to fetch 'em corn butt alien

paper ship mill coal blouses
gonna co-coax 'em with a fake
snake shake shake it

with a stir it
with a slur of the circling
whole kernel shebang

and what's that rising
moral mirage lope
no not in resignation

why it's weary ruth
furrow for her pillow
weeds the row tidier

than any herbicide's
silent violent
choke vote

weeds by the grinding
her old true teeth
in a new new dream

about the town wall
was a stranger bread
then how you bite down

comes keys
hauled to grape
oar by broken sea

calls in its cracking
back for tacky squirrel
whose jug bean maybe what

whose jank tail in its jitters
is fires for furlongs
is pulpits for puppets

is god's little eruptions
fur around fast cold shoat
as dog's a god adoze a dream

of lancer legs yip
of sharker teeth yip
nose holes odes hurricanes

IN KEY OF WISH RABBIT SINGS

to vermillion hats marooned
upon sentimental nails
scabbed some with seafoam

slouching loom
woofing cinnamon
churn that haunch crank and

fresher outsetless owlet swings
low loaf old toe mouth
cartoon cat bread neck

like this it's guillotine's
brethren light loot out
one wind mechanical

why joist bird o save me
suture stretch pants pleat
egress bucket galleon

trueler taller there are none
ladder ladder loves the dust
til it don't then up

now stooping
is it
kingly

else or i am goner
one gaghand down
wide-eyed wisdom

first joist bird alloy
sky salve slather
yr long and yr lovely

fernal gill throat furniture
undulant verve dent
frogstack neck trill

turtle winter pond
muck stack talk guinness
pinted ostrich throat cartoon

cept it's frog frog frog frog
fair will dark tree hotel
free crane neck spindle

let's up gas the couch that
let's going and yesterday
to some florida of moon now

where the living and dead play
whittled punctate
legbone golfclub whistles

talk mad cloudages
veined in heart attack light
rhythm of shit country tequila dreams

pup up on shine stone
suture bird ladder down
red the head red the eyes

by way of the blood dream
by terrible shake this infant stillness
son it's hotter than hiway milk mama

where if only we are good now
we'll one day leashless be
maddeners of sea

waves salt cake waves
rabbit upon rabbits
a chaos of leap feet

and footnoted hearts
drum solo freak freaks
gravid dust unsettling

why soon enough sleeps
yes soon enough sleeps
mmm soon enough sleeps

calls to question
why don't frame shudder
hangover clotheshanger that

light frozen conductored
into something like crane
dippin insides lures

insidious car lock coax
atom bomb erect out from
the eyeholes of a dead man

unpopular in his demise
as he was in whiffling life
ash to grass and may we be

moved through mannered
mulctless guts of muculent ungulates
no not some two stroke blare rooster

struttin like stone no
comet shit freak for a home
and the steamin cold shoulder after

ambulatory bivalve hopechest
from above any straight
line unshields its curls

and sadness grains
old shill shoal winsome
low high between cranes

impossible that one
lifting as they do the cornbread
and the county cataltyic picker too

gonna plant your chaff in awkward litmus
talk alphabet of socks now
frozen to weapon

on the line i have in mind
personal vintage aerial ladders
and to step 'em down nothing

but my eyes and fingers
the ones upon the others
the heart walks shy shed

the frog fly swallow swallow
the drunk pray burp only
the egg pulse cry beak

the diaphanous dark sick of it
slow crane the bucket up
from heartless well

prime a stately monster mind for real
soda water precious water freshest water
you yes this pulse mulled

you can of beets on the dash heart you
cardboard pizza by grease bled thru on the dash heart you
energy slump silo dick on the dash heart you

secondhand dashboard
dead gum blue
carry one cracked in the backseat

just in case sweet must
cathect an up ahead
looking back now that's

pure peril
passion play
endless white blood delight

annulled in
salt's empathic charge
can't seem cease

juicing fossils
in the neck twist of all
i did not know how say

these willowy risers say
this fig leaf tent vinyl sky
breakable when

beyond is for life
arrow hollow bone
borne upon regret's exhale

back when we barely knew
rudder from plough
or how to throat the sun

bunch of thistledown blown
thickest in wall meets wall
such faithful faithful fails

for wings unfurled
i find i stow ·
where skulls are

honey is
wrist and
ransom deep

HOODWINK AUBADE

morning tings the kissy face promise
of another nra 2x4 badass axe
stonin the mailbox faucet stonin

pamphlet paper prop plane crashland in
possession of no weakness and
with the rabbiting frequencies

and comin for you
you and yr sides
gonna gather 'em up scoop 'em

get a great hot australia fire
buncha lily blowhards
gonna gotcha melt that gunpile

but son have you every
considered the thing
bruising yr shoulder meat

from kickback like a milkcow
back in the day ever since yr a child
that's that tree wood

ignition grain the things'll burn
danger loser at the stocks
dray heave midnight sun

metal'll slow now slowcrawl
them pansy liver bursts
gonna stump around about masses

and eye-exed bled out
children but did you
everyway think what about if i

had been there i
would've killed the killer
before the killer killed see

fire gets so high god is
dancing like a rooski bear
and they stir glad oozing barrels

them buncha snowflakes
with the kitten hearts and water
color smiles crackrib huggin

like it's the new year
gonna rump it all into a cast mask see
east of jimmy carter clinton's face

and up for the crow cash mash
up just above the meltin melon eyes
between there throw them some worry

seed sinks in a little
that's for the acne scars
keeps the too pretty police back see

seed's the 2nd name
for magnet in bird day 1 7
crane parachutes goldener up there

feastin and echofootin peace signs
along the way up where the worry line
tv antenn goes for normal

peacey jimmy
cansaw billy
snuff it all with a vote

now when bullets get so high
i can't paperbill no ammo no more
snuff it all the way vote a dope

tater that nra stall a wart flet pam
take and paper drake it on to war
surest edges positively beaky

seed speed sniper insomnia
rake a spite sight peep
in failing chalk wall and

they wooled sisyphus stone in
and tantalus goad on see
pulp in like this that's a crash

back guarantee just this
side of immortality about
the worst you can expect

little lifting play to the paper edges
and that's fine fettle
for bowl shovel

your sugar stew through
on the daily steady
prop a crutchy stream threading

me call one among the icicle hunters
gatherers going around
just this side of stone frozen

'scuse me guest ghost out the mouth
may i harvest yr clear teeth
yr eaves' weep quartz show

and haul 'em back
somewhere where the weather
same inside as out

ain't hard larder left to count
when plosive is
pigeon splutterin out

from slumpin barn
a rouge tooth shot
across puke carpet

out from narrow grey
gappy gob damn methy
dan's devil on the leeside laugh

go ahead and ram them
those silence icicles as one
thread and ease 'em then

through yr eyelids
how's that feel
arctic cant effect

firing yr up deep down
sleep outside underneath the moon
mr diamond eyes

sparkle and dim cording
to the fuck it of the passing
woodsmoke or clouds

turn that up deep
pin in a bread jaw
sound felt from firmness

paper the truthity thump to it
call me sticker bagged
belong am among

hunters funners
protectors of family listen
either the dip i fell asleep with in

or the repeating function
on my dream arm moon diarrhea
unborn baby kicking heart

pigeon spasm all
up in neck this mine hear
about somebody breaks in

and it's me 'gainst the world
of war tactic in that fucked
vet zigzagging through my home

and i can react see quick enough can i
when the meth in himself
runnels them stairs

just this side of jet fuel oil
and i in the slow hill
of a 9 brew night

come to be this thing of
earth blood barber pole
in turgid subdigit reverse and i been

to baraboo how bout you
got close personal pretty up
with cranes there they

come at you with a purr
in their faces at a zigzag and
diesel glowplug eyeball

i couldn't see it
being humanly sighted
nothing but the green of the grass for me

but it's purr purr zig zig
and zag man that bug
beetle wading low wad way

under didn't stand a ground
peppercorn of chances it's almost like i can feel what
the loser beetle felt by sound

by the clack clack of
crane lips it's almost like
back when cranes were

coming up study this
tens of million ago
things got made out of

what was at hand
it's almost like a crane's some crazy
rickety blind baby mouse reed corn

bottlefed by the DT's sun and
i can relate to that scab it
rig it underwear stitching

calvin inclined
to tinklin on a logo
for a chevy

after all everywhere you
are hard you are soft
in a dream of killer bees

so these crane lips i don't know
mahogany tree split in two by
recent lightning chop

in the clack hands
of the baron at the bath
salts factory

i can't explain really
what it felt like to be
touched by that sound

the glowplug sear hush of it all
and i in this diesel utero rain wheat
trying to react gun cabinet key key

miss methvet gasfire craneclimbs
stairs blisters misfits mine and you gotta be
poorer than we are not to have that sneak mean

up unto the children i fess it's a nation
where hello is a punch a gut
and goodbye about the rackled same

everybody everwhere out on the snow yard now
bent gasp double wondering what
might come up and hopin for air down

go on and gawk about gun troll
when it happens again without
a dip in mine eyes

giving birth to
my own heart and i aztec thump it out
thrill and thrall it out my

rhythm hand throws vermillion snake
babies out to wolves
cinchin their circle blood-nicked

eyes don't play with no
slipknot talk to me about
the steaming fatted calf

about that beer bloat what cows
and no insurance walmart 38 hour a week
digesting everything in 203489 amazon stomach

now is that prime spit in
yr tum tum
or are ya just sappy to ghost me

near wild
snow yard
mahogany and struck

by the jerk pigeon
leafing a dead barn
weird with bird streaks i profess

one trash bird going over
it's like the sky
it crapped

only as i been shitting nra pulp now a time
the bicker yard stoned in castles of it
such that when the snow goes

the dogs to piss upon my passed pyramids
of nra toast
i am saying this

so you can picture this
voided pulp
meltless halfassed snowmen

and given how yellow i would eat
a grab of snow or swamp if i was you
dog throat yell on offwhite

and slumping like some
wicked rich dream
of a haystack way back

you can do it look up
to where the ropes went
and the sheaths and the shocks was luau'ed in

loose like this like that
like this spring arrives
a grease a goat

a vision time swims
pigeon freak splutter
seems some a broken pen son

ink seep stone
up river kicked all
ufo waffle by fleeing deer

iced eyes mine pooling
knowledgeable serious and slow holdy
as if long throat rope or leg of fish

comes to me
out of the dark underflow eternity
has it some electricity

jerks for release
pant leg with a puppy in it
sugar beats each teeth

janus as peach and pit
as if tucked up and out
one passionless ice hole

what there is to be afraid of
and it's sweet and it's rotten
dances like a dog does

whose only heater the table
scrap fading like bell's tight light
pattery musk in time cow says

i just jingle to proceed
me that docile cauliflower colander moo
retired to any antsy sandbox

where none might guess at
my records of repeat heats
my steadfast refusals

to hold on to
anything for longer
than times told

by holes
in a logic of pissin
precious everything away

YOUR ANCIENT
& FRANKLY BREAKING UNDERWEAR

yourself your skeleton's
a skewer so yr shoes
wear weird yourself

your buttered beef heart
yourself yr shrew soul
it's not waiting

for its own hartled start to calm
for phone's red light flashing
for blood's a vision to ez see by

in the budbeg watermarked motel of the self
in the nine miles east of gary
indiana of the self deep breaths now

so the hand don't tremble so
when retrieve letbloodlight message
if they didn't just breathe

just breathe animated sandpaper
breathe and hang up
beige phone

easily the temperature
of this beige room
beige room easily the temperature

you set it on
so much turtle truly
within your real reach

within your constant control
the soul the metered materials
you prat schist 'em every day

your six color socks your soul way
your clever clever cups
your soul way

shoot a crane
shoot your own soul away
the slaves in the southeast

heard lamentation salvo call
three loops above
the leaning shack i promise thee

faceless locust coinages all in a heft rain
three corkscrews around three
passes at scooping out gourd

one floor slick with great seed one
cork spent to loess's glee
bottle boat song tomb conch for

flotsam fly
and
me

leaning lack shack leans natch as breathing when
nails bald teeth jiggled from wild jaws
dealed sharpless by hungers hushed hungers hauled

when bones escutcheoned by callings' burnings
tri looped tri looped rued they
death is soon let it not be you

fettles into forgetting
why it happened so quickly
first candy then the roomy

exposed wire
interiors of the white
white cavern van

every oxygen extra in the movie of yr life
if constancy is a courage worth entertaining
craaaaaaaaaaaaaaaaaaaaanes

alighting as parachuters do upon the broken plains between
dispassionate threads of factory water and lucky beauty
faux lion mane we pat pretty parts dry with

ageing being about the unapologetic drying of the body
in public spaces so i am not so careful as i used
with the blinds east of gary a ways

stranger dew aloha to the low
mewl motel of me to the red
light flashing to the tune of

some sandy lost fossil message turning
in the gut at gary
and east some and

they do say a shell hosts
the ghost of the sea
in her gleaming winding stair ear forever

in receiver yellow violin style forever
in retrieval's calm claim cradled forever
unction junction function forever say

pump suspended and seeping
gauche but not forgotten
precipice eminence glacier

geyser garrulous paste
that broke thing with
wet mop hair my how

the stage gleams monotony
of the escalator being ten
times that of the stair

with a push
i invite you reader
old drunk friend

to sing into a pringles tube
of sea versus sod talkin
dial tone talkin

virgin verge
shirksome surge talkin
tubercular purrs

of the runt so inured to kicks
and with a swimmer's logic
and with the heat of the mother

for compass for sirocco radar
without eyes ever open even
arrives burning crusted where

the thwart was on where
the fix was in where
the teeth were out

where the claws where the claws
the boned muscle bustle man
bumping you out and

who drinks faster then and now
mouth or heart
narcotic milk

meting ease my purer old knock heart
the wool in the wedding bell
of my mouth let fall

call answers call
none alone long we
are one musical family

WESTFIELD

here we go
again again grandpa
harold william detra

one face over the other
try calling different
rain in the river and the rain

behind you i flew ah on yr maple
tapping missions in slush not quite
sinkin in dogbite cold melt snow

and the ol '26 yearbook
from iron mountain michigan
smells like a weddin of mosses still

and i am ya in there i the tap
you the sap i the fire you
the all night vigil i the syrup

you the basement steps i the creaking rising
with a fresh jar to take home grandma
cryin out why look who is here us running from

the dark brown chevrolet barely off it was not
beige or khaki it was like beige or khaki got to
bleeding to death deep deep dark brown yes

and with the drinking
and with the not quite laughing
and with the laughing like starting

a shit buick in cold
all my life that
question about what the lightning

snake of too
bright light through
your green seedlings did do

knocked you from
yr golf shoes in illinois
where you was teachin code

during the war daughter
betty ann up north of there
getting born

dial forward 30 years and
she changes her name to joy
dial back 30 and you wake up in

the hospital pants
still smoking zipper
walked straight

to cloth locked
no more zig
zag it was a time

it was unheard of
to throw
anything away

keeps for britches' patches
and you kepts in mind
forever after you was

part native american
saw that clear
in a green sweater swarm arm dream

knocked cold and cool
from the too furious bright
and sometimes i wonder

are we arrow or quiver
grate or drain
difference there negligible severe

one guzzles the other
almost grudgingly
swallowing the falling

the following to be held up
by ankle poke corn stalks
winter days or a day

before snow crane hill musics
the following to be becoming
from the milked july mist

from my first hearings of the cranes
through milked jug june mist even
with the pickle pickers

up the way
from michoacan
tarascan i remember one

hammered copper man new to a bike
legs mariposaing
shoulders stone laughing

while the bike
seemed to scent the rig rail
of yesterday's besotted moth jig way

and i remember her
in shade of elm
watching this sip bike try

and turning towards me
how empty lathe full i was
how empty full

quicksilver sliver bugle buried
in the bulging and red
dream of a hand

her arms tight over her waist
as tho to press firm there
might make fast

the tatters
of her
geography

but if you have laughter
so they say you
are never less compass

shotgun
marriage of
radish and raspberry and pine me

so small afraid all
times oh go big they
cash flute rope aria

twined thru musica
it was raining
so there was party

every song single
in a camel lintly
conjunto accordion wave

pumps a wash fertilizer
into the dry bean
crane word

things jump so
like a drunk
in a drunk gasp dream

heard sound takes yes
and licks us up into a shape
grandpa cussing out

hooks and slices
pumping ball after cracked ball
up the hill towards the lath

meant as flag
coffeecan meant for hole
great god big oaks to the right

elms corns birch pines
accordion crane mist coiling
calling all that shapely and

wings arcing from it
like a wave like smoke
like a sheet unfurled

wing arm tintype intimate
with not through mist
wing for a wardrobe oboe

call the folding ruler
with each click the map
of the mind unfolding

for i was safe
in the songs
for i was safe in yr cuss blasts

covered me
in cast slack rope
uncullings god damn it

all to hell i am under
there still under there
in steer and stow

from wobble card table after a party
the crumbs and the butts
set sail shudder at

anything measured
against their life
in flight

what you knew to be then didn't
of yr right life falling from yr ears
of butts and of crumbs

was like yr failing head
milked yr body
so thin percocet obsessed

grandma fretting
furrowed so face
wrinkles if if if

if stepped over edge
of one how far
that fore duck fall

turning winter
the cranes lifting
like parachutists falling

didn't make no sense
toward nebraska
and new mexico

or kiting over the ohio
for florida
where joy's yips

with the putter tomorrow promise
yr green rage and the too clean windows of
gordon's vodka under kitchen sink at 5 at 3

at 1 it's harder to tell where
cool opacity ends and
the burner gin jumper cable blood

begins she's another shaker
me her you
is it the ash after ya got

struck snowing through
our limbs forever first snow
and yr gone again

grandma doing the 9
and 1 and 1 one
full wheel spin

and the others two
tiny twists hardly touch
her arms in her gut in her worry

watches one eye squad car
crests the hill their toplights
on show patched cloths thick

mizzle eye she can see
the crumbs of snow revolve
in electric light and in mist and

dial they seem to 999
or some such
universal clarion

strop or strobe
the ropes of their flashlights
highlight and hold

in their pisses the butts
of snow swimming out
their slow shell lives

hands up for a pillow behind yr head
sir what doin sir and
do you know where you are

was just watching it snow and seein
if i could get a good
joke from the moon

gentle i was alien
full ham skull generous
pulses still

with their badges glinting
wild cat cold tongues with their authority
obnoxious author of stone

up sir and we'll
take you up the house
up to it you know where

you are i was just watching
the stars when the cloud furrow
moon when the cloud mustard

you made your kolache sick
with worry you could've froze
i was just watching moon

give piece by piece
its best west blest water it's capable
i am of holding it if briefly

of eating into it of an actual water eaten
by one moon shat by one
star luffing quench i see

spy again my origin
in among an old edible light whose
taste no taste a distancing

whose fighter flight lifer
whose rise parachutists lifting
whose water

gauzy meld light
sandwich life
to the points

of words and their slowback
roundings to a darkling vice
i sing to cast

in bronze and gold
and silver and iron
and pig lead and lion granite

and bash and bash it
and bash and bash it
until stars islands

under foot and i step
through myself
isthmus am

born to be bridging the itchin lonesome
them bastards had heavy guns
and flammable costumes

swished when they walked
as if stethoscope i had and then
miraged it cross strike a match

what's yr hurry ticking
snow sky old snow lagoon
through whose bottom

turtles line it button it
dream as seeds dream
first little smoke of green

and turning to rise spire
and rising again fly
flakes for foeless steppin stones

for golf balls smashed salt small
for i so hit the sweet spot why i
felt it felt what nothing at all

PURPLE MOUTH LIFE

so brief and the briefer
the purpler the ink
to lease at least

back in the day
where the idea was taste
lasted for a generation

in throat's insides
therefore cranes
epicurean fiends

therefore cranes
jealous worthy
info hiways

of tipple so guys
craned cranked themselves
a little each day

to maximize the wine
just as guys will
gear towards performance

missing by a tire swing
sagacious with raintar tannin
the point about life

a pigeon right at you
a bee right at you three tree bees
the ducking the dancing true

how you roll a holy lacquer gold
over reflex or duty's dayby
that's all that i might

swallow allow the same
urge coin of wine mudded
hourglass going dunno down

threads its traipse toes
mingled with conjecture
as per the yawning clown

as per the swell portico this
lamplight quaffable
most unbash

mimes a freshfruit
mine is too
attenuated peach lights

pressing pink and orange
against blue
penals of steel

grandpapa there
grouchin in his shark shoes
on in the corner there

proofin history
a matter of stretching
back from fishing

sound asleep sound
little flaps of lips his
cut down a coast

of forests in zanzabar
his neck trailin out
his pantleg his

out past the disappointment mailbox neck
his out past the twin oaks neck
out past the goldenrod

his out past the yellowrocket
his now you'll have to
see it with your mental neck

out beyond museum barn
whole county one
abandon sounds like a rainwet

pigeon slappin her blase freaked
blase freaked heart awake she
feebles touch bad luck barn

whose springruns shits never dug out last
whose roof cut gill prodigal whose
weathered roof's harelip slit

permits one bad banana
string of good day
light to ride

down floorwise and lifts
given springtime next and natural
damps of nowhere inviting

this one regal thistle up
for whose wide wide
cactus britches

and personal space
purple heart i writhe to vision
through sugarcubes

TOUCHSTONE BLUES

A tinnitus towards Aristotle's <u>History of Animals</u>

drop from above
animate reeds
animal cattails

vacationing astronauts
hanggliding hungover
do the fog parachutist

do gingerbeer strawbone
do the stepacross rooftop
antennafeet touchdown in

among drifterly meadowly glades
to bob to and through all tall grasses
taller bird queasy gait like grease

on an empty
excuse me y'all
yellow phlegm gut slide

touchstone stone garbled in
venture rate ain't fixed man
one snake for one stone try

and sometimes i dream
basalts for mirrors
just nothin to 'em

as per sightly shine
just the taste in yr mouth
says all who you are

and how and farmfrack hands
and ice shins and crookroad toes
and the hairs like filigree there upon

now you can cut into anything
can cut in and witness
satiation's green shoes

the bends to the circles
swelled by such hunger
secret traces the turns

the turfs the snails the snakes
to the thing's rounding days
last seen supper lesson spelling

little squint seed mat sips
little naked napkin frog
eye avalanche spilling

from gullet crop
for grists gutsy
stones pestley

pounders chips off
the old millstone
stones in the pathway

spin 'er dry
fulla wet jeans
looser change

spin in
the purgatory
of on the way down

one big bad bird
almost halfchosen what
gets bit and lever'd in

but none no
not chose
post peck gob lift and slide

gets locust hail personal fast
pounce pouch flinty fleur
gonna hopper you out

bark the rock bird in
kind precious test stone
to pull a possibly

changed life along
this here like a stove match
and see if you ersatz are or

steady toward the surface
water lords the promise
arisen by the held in

swimmer like a fountain
in ecstasy of breathing
some frenzy and some calmness

something steady rising
and needing to for life
in the hay the golden spends on light

go gold gold gold gold
go gold gold gold gold
go gold go go and see

if the glimmer people don't
gather their shitty glitz all
in plead weeds around

pleased be just ashed on by
your plutonic britch cloth
come true deet

on a campfire bark the touch
bird sends folk cold
called out to the edges of the seasucked earth

bark the rock one snake
for one touchstone the
one rudders the other

the human spine jerked sibilant
humane tongue split and
dragoning on in behind

this thing on thank you bird
became from snakes
yearned for skies

whose chill scales to feathers
lunged once whose need to
airtruck the cold dead is

beside the point
and shunt our deathrat echoes
in notches upon the diamond spine

half way down you rising
bird barf bird ark
ben frank kited key

the eating part it gets complicated
yes it does for no snake
worth agog wants go down bird

rather be pulled longer
by hunger than poledance
some triller's hollow leggo

in a cowboy lasso dream
when the lasso for motor
has a teenaged mind

sudden kite
waking feel what
it would be to carry up

something still quitting
its purpose down new to
float reverb revivals

the kite ache ate its string
anarchic as
a moon beam and

on what do you rise sir
why with hiss here cargo
extension cord writher

hiss golden
shandy opine
massager

ravel of writhe of rise of
do the pot boil sing inside
two exits down

the road and you
ain't nobody
your number sand

and your last
name trashed grass
allure of the road

cradled in zero
prosper in untime
blind willie johnson

died on a floor
in a broken house no
there wasn't one thing

recognizable as a thing
in there and all of it
touched totally touched by rain

bird bard willie
broke back up around
this bowl of sky

hey with writher still in
won't you sand a sandy glassy above
whip it froth wise side to side

until the thermal yanks
easy as pull a string you get gone
seasonal call purl wet pebble echo

tunnel and tongue in the ear
of the herniated sleeper
ah the people roust out then

sure do scurry gummed pigmeat
unstudied in their bowels bending
bows down their froggy legs

it's a shit gait for truly
raw ghost melon old dog gasp
uncareful now between thighs

wiped their
ass with a chafe crow
and the caw hangs on way to rot trot

their only burden themselves
their only burden themselves
their only burden themselves

but fearless at last
of ankles extinguished
and rolling out puff puff to where

the grass eye high here
see haughty nearly or trusting chin back
sun shave wait on a stub

brakelight come on in a toe
pain chums a switch has that
cusp be damned cup the contour

quality stoop quick now
do your best
natural gas metal dino bird

and lift this touchstone
maybe still warm
from the internals

of sky swept bird
go on now and praise
over thine debt head belt

the bloodran boxer wins
and gods deny gods
that's the human in 'em

but can you blame
the voyeur
for mimesis eyepoke

in a minute
it won't be possibly to say
if it's your hand heat

going in or the gullet's
gradual residual minstrel
going out or the sun's

unrelenting
hocus of the
two three

not that
far from
the 4eye heart

this hottish heart of stone
cooling sounding
worth a toss

but you gambol instead it
held high wild high turtle head hands
and mooseblood sun so

sings in you
tips your head back
tipples to dregs absolute

afternoon red
yarn let with a large green yodel
let out your own in crane

for nothing wild inside stays
embrace yeah by flung speech
certain songlike qualities

tap untrap say wild thing
stage yr worth is largely
what you at large come up upon

now did ya have hand
or knee or the rumble in yr
pastnoon on the wheel on the way

now press real hard here
and stay pull it either is
or it isn't you either

are or you are not
in a judgment louder than name
tell it to me slow quest first

fingers in mouths
to keep from off fall
all the while chanting

best we can
with a hand
at the mouth

up a little mutton fond ways
up over dry gulch yonder
can't be much long now

horizon in a case
gun or pool cue
the precious finality dawn does

back out on a busted wander
out over clod hill hair wild
the wind o it oceans what's solid

strong enough today to lean in
closest thing to a wild wing
your collar at your mouth now

then in and you wet it
when moves against you again
according to the willy decker tapes of wind

when you've forgotten later
your lover's tongue
mining for the salt

for champ ball of your heart
for the river deeper bankless ruined
for the dream of your longest bone

for your bone's
aside of the afterlife story
for your bone's windfall will

i wish to be a dowser obnoxiouses the one
and i a tool to scrag for water too and i
to jink for gold and i to crowbar taters

now place your awl of it here
'mands the last and longest now
punctate like you're drowsing

at the wheel at intervals now
passion drags and strobes now
place your yellow finger here

your other there now
and there and gettin here
your sorry mouth

at this end cheer now
let nothing fund the other
let nothing come between

you ar..i the free song
blows out like obsidian
into the astonished heart

of the hearer
lover thrown
down cast back now

wing snare hair now
snake skin scroll now
whose meticulous

suggestions by weather
time and sweat
simmer to bruises now

and what is the word for
the horse steps the grape now
for the beard of ants

frothing from nowhere
like shook beer
how about the gnomic farrier

shoes with champagne
flutes only
smashing one

crystal shower
after another ants
like time ants like fat now

inside the bone now
hollow's playback
o haul's feel prom

call it the woodtrick blues
called down to fawn
upon the ghost whose spit

dials spots 999
upon baby
rides forked

and bending right along
whose tapered and
willowing fingers reach

for a dowser in a duel
untwine wide peace now
toward the 1tree we must need now

back the ears clean bring
gobbed the sight unburns please
our dead alright unmoaned arising

from muskrat atolls
in the radiant clothes we
once kept for rainy day prodigals only

WHY EAT WHY KILL

how hunger boy
mercer must you
brain crane lay

over lap one
dream broom
person starved

down chaff
rain pencil
shaving ego

peck of
pimpled flesh
on fire

eat burnt crane
eat burnt crane
eat burnt crane

who your gods then
while you wait for the soup
bird to unshade yr life

in who the cleated teeth
of rain
in mist

in whom the fired
sibilant remnants
a passing

storm's little
unsuccessful denials
of fire

inside every song
another song
fruit teaches this

white sun flesh
the seed at the breast
thread wrestled button the

crane
burnt
eaten

can't stack a day's
strength a night's
rest at the unravel hotel

truly hungry fools
dream too but
not of confluences

not of gardenias
not of pedigrees
not the stony feats

of insomniac sentinels
mothered by
the killing maze

milk like junk wool
milk like gauze
milk like hesitancy

might as well
eat your own cane
god and crawl

THRU WHOM INN WHOM:
MIGHTY THANKS TO

Monica Detra, William Detra, Linda Detra, R Smith, Erin Kavanagh, Meggan & Eddy Meisegeier, Angus & Rosy & Pippin Meisegeier, Joy Detra, Jane & Bob Detra Davenport, Pam Carazo, Larry Matuszewski, Mara Brown, William Pollett, Ryan Ridge, Jason Barrett Fox, Steve Timm, Shari Bernstein, Joyelle McSweeney, Johannes Goransson, Scott McWaters, Deb Davidovits, Tommy Dolph, Matt Harle, Eric & Ivet Parker, Mark & Jim & Eva Schultz, David Floyd, Warner Moore, Stephanie Ray, Ashley Durant, Giorgio Colombo Taccani, Hal Crimmel, Molly Heller, Joel Brouwer, Michael & Marilee Wutz, Tom & Kyra Hudson, Greg Brownderville, Nate Parker, Erica Revak, Chet Weise, Linda Harrison, Tim Earley, Emily Wittman, Craig Pickering, Forrest Gander, Jason Busse, Charlie Parr, Courtney Craggett, Jan Verberkmoes, Heidi Lynn Staples, Ander Monson, Don Revell, Sandra Simonds, John Pursley III, Adrian Kien, Sarah Blackman, Shelly Taylor, Scott Hunter, Ashley Chambers, and Jerry Goldberg.

And especial thanks to the empathic-wise Baobab team: Christine, Laura, and Danilo.

ACKNOWLEDGMENTS

Special thanks to the editors of the following journals where many of these poems, in different shapes and sounds, first appeared: *Academy of American Poets, Poem-a-day; Entropy Magazine; Action, Spectacle; Diode; Painted Bride Quarterly; Southwest Review; Interim; Yolabusha Review; The Condensery;* and *Tagvverk.*

Abraham Smith's recent publications include *Insomniac Sentinel* (Baobab Press, 2023), *Dear Weirdo* (Propeller Books, 2022), and *Bear Lite Inn* (New Michigan Press, 2020). Away from his desk, he improvises poems inside songs with the Snarlin' Yarns; their records *It Never Ends* (2023) and *Break Your Heart* (2020) were released on Mississippi's Dial Back Sound. He lives in Ogden, Utah, where he is associate professor of English and co-director of Creative Writing at Weber State.

Insomniac Sentinel's headers are set in Moret, a serif display type family inspired by 20th century European sign painting.

The body is set in Cormorant Garamond, a serif font developed by Christian Thalmann. While this project was heavily inspired by Claude Garamont's immortal legacy, Christian did not use any specific font as a starting point or direct reference for the designs. Most glyphs were drawn from scratch; when he needed guidance on a specific character, he searched for the term Garamond and skimmed through the results for a general impression.